SOUNDS of Silence

REGINA L. PEEPLES

Published by Jawbone Publishing Corporation

1540 Happy Valley Circle, Newnan, GA 30263

Printed in the United States of America

ISBN 1-59094-251-5

The characters and stories cited in this book are real. For their privacy, however, their names and some of the significant details have been altered.

Sounds of Thanks to My A-Team

There's no I in Team, and without you my A-Team, I couldn't have made this project possible

Acknowledgments

Roll Call……

My God~For entrusting this great assignment in my fragile, yet humbled hands. I wanna make you SMILE!

My Husband~Quentin{Peep} Thanks for supporting me and allowing me to live out my Purpose, Dreams and Passion. I love loving YOU!

My Children~Teron and Quentin for sharing me with others and truly understanding my Life's Purpose. Dream BIG!

My Mother & Chief Intercessor~Gloria{Sweets}For giving me LIFE, Faith, Jesus, and HOPE.

My Family~Extended & Expanded Thanks for your love, support and most importantly prayers.

My Spiritual Leaders~Apostle Dannie Williams & Dr. Precious Williams "For teaching me Jesus really can heal me everywhere I hurt."

My 1st Responders~My MMT Sisters: Betty Thomas, Twila Dyous & Yolanda Presley. Ladies, thanks for your continuous Empowerment, Encouragement & Enjoyment of sharing the gift of YOU to my life.

My Friends~Thanks for always being there for me. Every woman needs a safe place to bleed a quiet place to scream, friends, to dress her wounds. She needs the support of sisters who won't cringe at the honest truth, who are willing to walk by her side, who will listen to her stories and who will offer balm to heal her wounds. Thanks for being YOU to me.

My Supporters~Special thanks to Howard Dixon and Family and Citadel of Hope Ministries for selecting me for the Dolly Dixon Success Scholarship.

My Personal Motivator~Ambassador Barry Myers Thanks for always watering my purpose and pushing me into my destined place. You truly are a God send.

My Graphic Designer—Davyn Riley, Silverline Graphic Design 10123 US Hwy 441 Leesburg, FL 34788. Thanks for adding your creative touch to this project!

My Editor~Shirley Daniels, Write it Right! Fruitland Park FL. Thanks for keeping all my I's dotted and T's crossed.

My Sheroes and Heroes~ Ann, Drew, Jade, L'Dionne, Maria, Mia, Michelle, Rita, Samantha Clark, Shearlie Mae, and Stephanie. Thanks for trusting me with your secrets, scars, silence and incredible stories.

My Publisher~Swanee Ballman, Jawbone Publishing Corporation. Here we grow again, thanks for all your help with making this project complete.

My fellow Readers~Thanks a million for your support of this project. Let's break the Sounds of Silence

Special Dedication

In Loving Memory of

Mrs. Zsanelle "Nelly" King-Teamer

My Dearest Cousin Nelly, you indeed have received your Beauty for ashes, Oil of joy for your days of mourning, a Garment of praise for the spirit of heaviness, and for your shame you have received Double honor. Instead of confusion you are now rejoicing in your portion, now everlasting JOY shall be forever YOURS.

You're forever in my heart.

Until we meet again.....Rest in Paradise

Table of Contents

Preface

Chapter 1: Sounds of Silence

Chapter 2: Sounds of ME, "My Silence" and I

Chapter 3: Sounds of Rape

Chapter 4: Sounds of Truth

Chapter 5: Sounds of Innocence

Chapter 6: Sounds of SUPERMANN

Chapter 7: Sounds of Love

Chapter 8: Sounds of Sex, Lies, and Family Secrets

Chapter 9: Sounds of Pain

Chapter 10: Sounds of Forgiveness

Resources

PREFACE

Silence is a girl's loudest cry~unknown

I was gazing into the eyes of a little 9-year old girl who had just broken her silence as I stood there in mine. How could this little girl be freed? What could I do for her? I knew exactly what she felt and would face for the rest of her life. But I stood there like a deer staring into coming headlights. I had the power to help this girl run to safety in a flash, but was stuck in Fear not knowing where to start or what to say. Once again my voice was silenced because of fear no one would listen to me. That day I decided never to keep silent again about sexual abuse. I vowed to tell my story and speak up and out about sexual abuse every chance I could.

For those who really know me, know that I'm not a morning person. My family lives a rather active life so whenever I get to sleep in, I take full advantage of it. Especially on a Saturday morning which happens to be my personal mental health day. One Saturday morning I found myself lying across my bed well after 11 o'clock, and I didn't want to move from this rather comfortable position. I realized the doorbell or phone hadn't rung, the kids hadn't knocked on the door, nor had the dog barked. No birds were chirping outside my window or anyone cutting their grass on this peaceful Saturday morning. It was a picture perfect moment filled with silence. As my head slowly lifted off the pillow, I suddenly thought, this is what total silence feels and sounds like. That moment was a very peaceful sound and feeling. But the more I thought about it, peace isn't what I felt. I soon related the silence to that of sexual abuse victims. Immediately I jotted down "Sounds of Silence" on the first piece of paper I found as I forced myself out of bed.

In that silent moment a thousand thoughts filled my head. But I could clearly hear the title of this my second book. This is what's heard in a sexual abuse victim's life—Complete Silence. The flood lights of my soul were turned on, and as I thought about the Sounds of Silence I knew that the world was filled with people whose stories would never be told. People like the man I met one day after a speaking engagement who shared his painful story with me.

Or people like Jade whose story made the hairs on my neck stand up; thinking if I've heard one story about sexual abuse— I've heard them all. Hearing Jade's story and looking in her big beautiful blue eyes I knew she would forever keep her silence so I decided to release, Sounds of Silence. For all those victims that haven't had the right to remain silent for all these years. Some who've been placed on an emotional probation or worst, faced with silent life sentences because of their abuse.

Sounds of Silence is for YOU….

The young boy whose mother left him home alone with a predator disguised as a babysitter.

The young girl whose father forces her to have sex with him frequently.

The naive teenage girl who simply wanted a ride home, but was brutally raped by multiple football players.

The mother who knew her daughter was being molested by her live in boyfriend, but chose his love over her daughter's safety.

The 12-year old girl who lost her virginity to her favorite Uncle Joe, and now her family is forcing her to have an abortion.

The young man who just wanted to be one of the guys. But secretly struggles with his sexuality because his uncle raped him as a little boy.

The little girl who has to keep the family secret so her father won't be sent to prison. The beautiful young girl who died one night in her grandmother's arms after her grandfather ferociously took her precious virginity.

The confused prostitute on the street corner, so willing to give up her body for $20 because someone took her innocence for free years earlier.

That run-away child who is in search of LOVE—because everyone who said they loved him or her only hurt them.

Those whose stories and voices will never be heard because they overdosed on drugs trying to numb their inner pain.

Injustice anywhere is a threat to justice everywhere

Dr. Martin Luther King Jr.

SOUNDS
OF
SILENCE

Can you Imagine?

- Being a little 8 year old girl who could barely write her own name to identify herself at school. And yet her innocence is gone in a moment by someone she trusts to take her to the restroom or store.
- Being a 12-year old girl whose body is going through puberty and now she's getting the eye of older men, her grandfather to be exact.
- Having to pretend your menstrual cycle is on so he will stop touching you "down there." The only time he stops touching you is when he feels the maxi pad or tampon between your young fragile legs.
- Seeing a Playboy magazine at the age of 8 and no matter what you do, the urges of pornography still haunt you at 38.
- Being an 8-year old child sitting in a classroom trying to learn fundamentals that will carry you through the rest of your life. Instead, you have to pretend that last night your daddy read you a book as you fell asleep. In reality he came into your room only to please his lustful thoughts and habits. Causing you to replay this nightmarish story in your head instead of innocent 8-year old sweet dreams.

These are the reasons I decided to write Sounds of Silence. For the countless victims who have yet to break through their silence of shame, pain, and guilt.

Sexual abuse is a Silent Killer of the SOUL

Dr. Betty Mitchell

Chapter 1 Sounds of Silence

Our lives begin to end the day we become silent about the things that matter.

Dr. Martin Luther King, Jr.

After releasing my 1st book, *Inward Scream,* I began to hear so many stories of sexual abuse, incest, molestation, and rape. I had numerous people breaking their silence for the very first time with me. We spent hours discussing our issues, and finally figuring out why we react to situations totally differently from others. Talking with other survivors gives you a sense of normalcy. To know they trust me with their stories and now the telling of it; is indeed humbling.

As I listened to the stories of both male and female victims; near and far, rich and poor, young and old, and from all races and cultures; I was in total shock. It soon became evident that so many people shared in the common pain that for years I kept well hidden. Like others, I too was fearful and believed the biggest lie of them all that I was the only victim. Within my family, circle of friends, community, church, job, and yes, even the world.

As unique as a child's DNA matches its parents, so are the traits of sexual abuse in a victim's life. Traits of Fear, Guilt, Shame, Confusion, Condemnation, and Trust issues are just a few of the common traits of abuse. We can exchange stories of our Emotional Secrets, Struggles, Scars, Strength, and Silence for hours. Although our looks are different, our silent voices of pain are the same.

I soon realized as I heard more and more stories that a majority of these stories would never be released. So I embarked on this incredible journey to re-tell the painful stories of others in hope of helping other victims, prevent new incidents of sexual abuse, bring awareness and break the silence of this taboo social issue.

I was sexually abused from the ages of 8 to 15. Unfortunately, for 7 years; the perversion of men led to so many things in my life. Things I'll never quite understand, leaving me to sometime still question..... Why Me?

Over the years I've personally struggled with extreme trust issues, battled with low-self-esteem, fear, guilt, promiscuity, anger, confusion, shame and deep emotional pain just to name a few. It has taken me years to finally accept who I really am. That little innocent 8 year old girl staring back at me in the mirror through the eyes of a now 38-year old young woman and be okay with both.

Today I Boldly and Freely announce to

the world, I Am Regina L. Peeples, a

Victor of Sexual abuse,

not a Victim!

I broke the seal on my own Sound of Silence archives on Sunday, January 14, 2007. The sound that ranged from the depths of my soul set me FREE instantly. I was like a mother in labor preparing for that last painful push. Although the pain was excruciating it was necessary for the birth to be completed. It's been said that during birth, you are as close to death's door as possible. After having two children, I agree with that statement; be it an old wives tale or not. The moment I broke my silence, I literally died. Not in a natural sense, but emotionally and spiritually. The person I once was, died that day. I died to my flesh, feelings, emotions, guilt, shame, condemnation, unforgiveness, and fear.

I never knew this journey would lead me to become an published author, sexual abuse advocate, or even a inspiration to others. I simply yielded to the voice of God that January day, and broke through 25 years of my own pain, shame and silence. So I know what Sounds of Silence really looks, feels, and sounds like.

Whether you've been touched once or once too many times, know this: you aren't alone in this journey. There is Healing, Help, Hope, and Freedom for you. Hear the "Sounds of Silence" being broken one story at a time throughout the pages of this book.

I'm for Truth, no matter who tells it.

I'm for Justice, no matter who it is for or against.

I'm a human being, first and foremost, and as such I'm for whoever and whatever benefits humanity as a whole.

Malcolm X

<u>"More than A TOUCH"</u>

When I was 9 years old instead of "playing" with

Barbie and Ken, I was introduced to Playboy magazines ***instead.***

It has taken the blood of Jesus to get these images

out of my ***head.***

Leaving perversion's DNA all over my internal ***being.***

Making me second guess that Woman I'm now ***seeing.***

Keeping secrets my soul wasn't built to ***bear.***

All while being told I love you and I ***care.***

Living in the confinements of internal walls of guilt

and ***shame****, unable to even recognize my own* ***name.***

Which actually means ***Queen.....***

the Little Girl in the woman, just longing to ***scream!***

SOUNDS

OF

ME, MY SILENCE & I

Chapter 2 Sounds of Me, My Silence & I

I am not what happened to me, I AM what I choose to become.

Carl Jung

There once lived a little feisty girl named Regina. She lived in a small town called Wildwood Florida in a tiny but modest home near the railroad tracks. She was a daddy's girl. She was his only child at the time, and he adored her. Everywhere he went, she tagged along and became his shadow's shadow. Even when he went to the bad places, she would tag along. That is until she told her mama all about him drinking from that can with the blue bull on it. A can of Mr. Pibb soda had always been a favorite for both him and her. To see her daddy drinking from this funny can was a story for her to tell her mom, or so she thought. Her daddy laughed it off, but she quickly learned to keep "their" secrets. This wouldn't be the last secret she would learn to keep.....

She was also the only grandchild and niece on her mother's side of the family. Quite naturally, she was spoiled rotten. It would be at least five years before the arrival of the next grandchild. Until then, she got everything her little heart desired. Like any little spoiled girl, she had lots of toys to play with but treasured only a few things. Her brown Teddy bear, her purple bike, her Miss Piggy Doll and yes that record player on which she constantly listened to the story of Robin Hood. She even got to choose when and if she attended the elite private school her dad and grandmother sacrificed to pay for her to attend.

At the age of 7, her world as she knew it would drastically change. Her parents divorced and she stayed with her mama. Her dad was no longer there to tuck her in at night, read her bedtime stories, or even play a game of "skin the cat" with her. She saw her daddy often but not as much as she'd wanted and would eventually need to.

One summer a close family member took something very valuable and important from her. He stole her innocence and identity. He hid her innocence behind their secret and her life would never be the same. She was just 8 years old when a trip to the corner store exposed her to his semen as he pretended to let her drive his car. Like most sexual abusers, he used her innocence, vulnerability, naiveté, and of course her father's absence to his full advantage. While lavishing her with candy, gifts, toys, and treats in exchange for her complete Silence. She didn't know what had happened to her or what that stuff was between his legs. Nor did she ever told a soul what he did. Her silence was exactly what he wanted. It was a secret code for him indicating he had groomed her quite well.

Soon after that eventful summer, her 9-year old eyes and soul would be exposed to hard core pornography. The images still haunt her mind to this very day. The louder she screamed for HELP, the more her family's secrets were forced to be kept silent. Once again forcing her to keep Silent even though she didn't have the right to. By the time she was 12 years old, the world of molestation would become her new mental address. Being repeatedly molested by a family friend for the next three years of her life became the norm for her. When she spoke up about what was happening to her, she was told to keep silent and not to tell anyone about it. Her truth would cause too many problems for too many people. So she remained silent for 25 years.

Forcing her to live in a dysfunctional emotional place. The place where secrets lived and were buried alive, silently screaming internally for an escape. The place where a little girl was forced to become a woman too soon. The place where her inner trust was forever shattered. The place where she longs to know, why did they chose me, my innocence, my life, and my virginity? The place where a girl wants to remember her very "first time" no matter how good or bad it was. The place where she totally forgot about it because it no longer represented a special occasion to her. The place where you lose a few good memories in order to forget all the bad ones. The place where everyone is a suspect in your mental lineup, and you no longer trust anyone. It's this place that causes you to build walls so tall and wide no one gets into your emotional "gated" community.

After 25 years of total silence she, like 1 in 3 women, boldly raised her hand and repeated these common five words "**IT HAPPENED TO ME TOO.**" Only this time she kept telling it to anyone who would listen. Because of her boldness many others have shared their story with her, breaking their Silence for the first time too. Within the pages of "Sounds of Silence "you will read about other Survivors of Sexual Abuse and Assault, Incest, Molestation and Rape. May their stories inspire you to break your own Silence and live whole, happily and freely ever after.

For to be free is not merely

to cast off one's chains,

but to live in a way

that respects and enhances

the freedom of others

Nelson Mandela

SOUNDS

OF

RAPE

Chapter 3 Sounds of RAPE

"No, my brother!" she said to him. "Don't force me! "

2 Samuel 13:12

Hidden Scars

"Lord, why now? It's been over twenty-five years. How can something so simple and innocent unleash such harsh memories? What could I have done differently? How can I explain to my husband of twenty-seven and a half years that a simple little gesture made during horseplay has me delving back into my past?" One incident in particular that has caused me much grief and hostility has resurfaced. I am saved, sanctified, Holy Ghost filled, and called into ministry; yet I had been in captivity for over twenty-five years. Held against my will, with what appeared to be no way out. It still amazes me how one incident can alter your life forever and hold you captive for as long as you allow. Rape is one such incident. I honestly thought that I had been totally delivered and set free of the negative effects of rape, over my life. It had taken me several years to get to this point, now I realize that I had only suppressed the memories. Memories of a time that I had never wanted to revisit.

Rape is a crime of control. It's about dominating a situation, having power over another person. It leaves you feeling dirty, guilty, hurt, and angry. If you stay angry long enough, that anger can turn into hatred. At least that's what happened to me. I can't believe I'm feeling this way. This entire confrontation has found its way back into my mind and I'm fighting hard for it not to re-enter my heart. How can I allow this stuff to consume my mind again? I went to bed last night with it on my mind and I've awakened to it this morning. I guess I've never really dealt with these issues. "Lord, what am I to do with this?" All I hear is "write it down." Rape also takes away your trust of other people. I had to put forth a special effort to spend time with my husband, today. These feelings that I'm having are trying to push me away from the only man that I've given my heart to, but I will not allow that to happen. James 4:7 tells us to resist the devil and he will flee. My marriage bed is blessed and undefiled. My husband is a very loving, kind and gentle soul. I truly believe that he is the one and only man that God has designed, especially for me; and I thank God for him, daily.

A flash back to the past…

It was June 1977, my sophomore year of high school. It was a very warm afternoon, a few days before the class of 77' s graduation. I had not gone to school that day because my fourteen-month-old son was ill. Shortly after noon, there was a knock at the door. I had just laid my sleeping baby in his bassinet and proceeded to answer the front door. I opened the door and a guy whom I'll refer to as Max was standing there with a big smile on his face. "Hey girl, I just stopped by to check on ya since I didn't see ya in school today, but 'huh' you look good to me." "Thanks I'm fine. I didn't go to school today because by baby was sick and running a fever." "Good cause you shonuff look fine." "Yeah right." I was dressed in a pair of shorts and a tube top. "Ya know, graduation is just around the corner so, where's my graduation present?" At this point I realized that he had been drinking but felt that it was ok because he was a long time friend, almost like family. We chit chatted about general day to day stuff for a while and then he started acting kind of weird, asking about his graduation gift again. I told him I didn't have a gift for him and besides, graduation was still a few days away. "Oh, you got what I want for graduation and I want it now." His statement along with the look in his eyes kind of put me on edge and I asked him to leave.

"You know Max I think you've had a little too much to drink. You really should go now." "What you mean, I'm not going nowhere until I get my present." As I started to show him to the door, he grabbed me from behind and lifted me off the floor. I was caught off guard and started fighting to get free of him. My mother's room was just to the left of the front door and we wrestled as he carried me into my mother's bedroom. Somehow, he got my hands pent underneath my body as he pushed me down onto my mother's bed. I continued to fight, using my knees until he overpowered me and proceeded to rape me. He was like a crazed stranger, continuing to abuse me until my baby awakened and started screaming. I don't remember how he left. What I do remember is how my head seemed to be spinning as I sobbed uncontrollably.

How could I have been so wrong in my judgment? I thought he was my friend. He left me feeling dirty, guilty, ashamed, and confused. How could I have allowed someone to overpower me like that? I could not tell anyone. I mean what would people think? After all, I was only sixteen with a fourteen-month-old baby. All I could think to do was take a hot bath. I washed and scrubbed my body over and over again but I was unable to wash away the feelings of guilt, hurt, and anger. I changed my mother's bedding and spent the remainder of my day on an emotional roller coaster ride. Why would someone whom I considered to be a friend, violate me and disrespect my mother's house? Me, the victim, yet again. I had been sexually molested as a child and have had countless sexual advancements made towards me by men of various ages. One guy had told me that just watching me walk turned him on and made him want to do things to me. Another guy physically chased me and made sexual advancements towards me because he said my smile turned him on and made him feel like I had wanted him. "How crazy is that?" I've always been one to smile and speak to others, male and female alike. I had been taught that it doesn't cost anything to speak to people and smiling just came naturally. I never wore skimpy clothes in order to get extra attention. I just wore what I like. With an hourglass figure, I got much more attention than I ever desired.

When I returned to school, a couple of days later, Max's brother came up and said "My brother told me y'all were together the other day," as if it was consensual. I asked, "did your brother also tell you that he raped me?" Needless to say, my day didn't go very well. When I passed Max during class changes, he looked at me and spoke with what appeared to be a little smirk of satisfaction, on his face. The hurt deepened and I grew angrier. I didn't function well for several days. All I could think of was how I would get my revenge. After that dreadful day in 1977,

I didn't speak to Max again for at least ten years. I graduated from high school in 1979, had gone on to college, graduated, gotten saved, married and had other children when I felt that my day of redemption had finally come. My mom received a phone call stating that Max had been shot and was in critical condition. Mom appeared to be quite distressed as she repeated the details of Max's injuries to me.

The family was terrified and requesting prayer for his recovery. Apparently, my response shocked us both. Mom cringed as I doubled over in laughter. Praying for a miracle on Max's behalf was nowhere near my mind or in my spirit. The only thoughts that had crossed my mind were Max had finally gotten what he'd deserved. After all those years, it had finally happened, but for whatever reason, my retribution didn't feel like I had imagined. I can't explain how I felt but I was like someone who had gone mad, laughing one minute and crying the next.

My mother was horrified but she knew that something had to have truly gone wrong in order for me to react in such a shameful manner. In a stern voice she asked, "Girl, what's the matter with you?" Max is lying in the hospital fighting for his life and you think it's funny?" When she realized that I was crying, her expression became one of sympathy and concern. Even then, I didn't want to tell my mother what had happened, but she being the person that she was, wouldn't let up. She continued to press me with question until I couldn't take any more. So, at the risk of destroying a lifelong friendship between our mothers and a relationship between Max's mom and my cousin, I finally gave in. Through tears of hurt and shame, I told my mother that Max had raped me all those years ago. My mom's reaction surprised me a little. She got upset and wanted to know why I had kept this information from her and for such a long time. Weeping as I spoke, "Mom, I didn't want to rip the family apart or destroy your friendship with Ms. Lena." Through tears of her own, my mom said "Look, you are my child and you are more important to me than any friendship. I'm so sorry that I wasn't there for you. Don't you know how much I love you and how much you mean to me?" "Yes Mom, I know you love me and I'm sorry I didn't come to you for help."

Trauma is an emotional earthquake

JoanHunter

We continued to talk and Mom wanted to know what could be done about this situation now, to make it right. I told her I just wanted to let it go and get on with my life. She respected my wishes and we never spoke of it again. At this point, I felt a need to tell my husband what had happened to me; so, through a little nervous tension, I gave my husband a very brief version of my past rape experience. He responded like most husbands probably would have. He got angry and wanted to hurt a man that was already struggling for life. Of course, he wanted to know more but I told him, I simply couldn't talk about it. He could have pressed the issue but out of love and respect for me, he chose to just let it go.

Later that night, I prayed and asked God to forgive me for rejoicing over Max's misfortune. It was hard but I also asked God to heal his body and give him a second chance at life. After surgery and several months of therapy, Max recovered. Over the next few years, I avoided him as much as possible. I had only seen him in passing, once or twice over a period of about five years or so. Then almost a year and a half ago, I came face to face with him. He walked up to me in the lobby of Shands Hospital, in Gainesville Florida.

I froze in my tracks and fear tried to take hold of me as Max slightly raised his arms in what appeared to be an attempt to hug me. I don't know what he saw on my face but in my spirit, I had begun to call on Jesus. "Thank God," Max stopped with his arms slightly bent at his waist as he dropped his hands to his side and asked how I was doing. I'm not sure but I think I responded by saying "I'm blessed." Then he asked "what are you doing up here?" "I'm (pause) "visiting a friend." He proceeded to tell me about his nephew being in the hospital. After an exchange of very few words, he said "it was good seeing you." I said

"Yeah; I pray that all goes well for your nephew." Then we parted and went our separate ways. I thanked the Lord for bringing me through a very awkward moment and allowing me to face my fears.

During the process of my writing this story, I hit some rough spots, stopped writing for several months and under direction of the Holy Spirit, I started writing again in January 2010. As I was praying to become a writer, on the level of my favorite Christian Fiction writer, Vanessa Davis Griggs, the Holy Spirit spoke to me and said, "It would never happen unless I complete this work which I started." My husband whom I had never shared the details of my rape with, came across my manuscript and read a very small portion of it before getting angry and putting it down. However, that occurrence opened up the doors of communication for us talk about his feelings as well as my own. Although it's been over 30 years, I still find it hard to talk about. After we talked, it felt like a weight had been lifted off of my chest and my husband encouraged me to finish my story.

Writing my story has been very therapeutic. I could feel the hand of God as he pulled me out of hiding and brought me to that place of peace that surpasses all understanding. I have sought the Lord and he has revealed unto me and confirmed that I have one finale step to take in order to bring closure to this chapter of my life. To those who read my story, I pray that it will give you strength and courage as you seek God to bring closure to your own. Thank you for caring and be blessed.

Courageously written by: Evangelist Annette M. Peterkin

The past is our definition. We may strive with good reason,

to escape it, or to escape what is bad in it, but we will

escape it only by adding something better to it.

Wendell Berry

SOUNDS
OF
TRUTH

Chapter 4 Sounds of Truth

Sexual abuse is defined as any involuntary sexual act in which a person is threatened, coerced, or forced to engage against their will, or any sexual touching of a person who has not consented. This includes rape (such as forced vaginal, anal or oral penetration), inappropriate touching, forced kissing, child sexual abuse, or the torture of the victim in a sexual manner.

The truth is speaking to us loud and clear through the lives of innocent boys and girls.

TRUTH IS……

- 1 in 3 girls will be sexually abused by age 18
- 1 in 6 boys will be sexually abused by age 18
- 52 girls and 150 boys are victims before abuser is arrested
- Less than 10% are prosecuted
- 66% of children don't tell anyone

A three-state study reported rape survivors under the age of 12 revealed the following about their offenders:

- 96% were known to their victims
- 50% were acquaintances or friends
- 20% were fathers
- 16% were relatives
- 4% were strangers

{Source: 10 facts about child sexual abuse about.com Nov 2011}

Can we hear the affects of Silence through these shocking statistics? Or will we continue to ignore the Sounds of Truth?

Contact Can Include:

- Fondling
- Obscene phone calls
- Exhibitionism
- Masturbation
- Intercourse
- Oral or anal sex
- Prostitution
- Pornography
- Any other sexual conduct that is harmful to a child's mental, emotional, or physical welfare

Whenever I'm talking about sexual abuse, I make it a point to dispel the myths about what's been referred to as "stranger danger." According to darkness2light.org, only 10% of abuse victims are victimized by total strangers.

Read|Between|The|LIES|

It is those we live with and love and should

know who elude us

Norman Maclean

It was a rough night; I had worked part of my 11pm-7am shift. I felt a migraine coming on shortly after I arrived to work. I knew I wouldn't make it seven more minutes, much less seven more hours, so I quickly found the charge nurse and asked to leave as soon as possible. I've suffered with bad migraines since I was a little girl often times needing shots to relieve my pain. I knew this was going to be a long night as I rushed home suddenly from work. At times the pain became so intense that I felt like I was hallucinating or having some type of out of body experience. A pounding head, blurry vision, along with a sweaty body are just a few of the common symptoms of a migraine.

I'm such a creature of habit that my family knew exactly when I would arrive home at exactly 7:30am. I expected them to be all tucked in bed fast asleep waiting the next day of school and work. As I walked in the house, there was an eerie feeling and dead silence that I immediately sensed. I just brushed it off as part of the worst migraine I'd ever had. By this time, I could barely see out of my right eye. I fumbled around in the dark in search of a few ice packs and towels to place over my throbbing head. Being very careful of my steps so I wouldn't wake my daughter, I tipped toed around like a mouse.

By now the pain of the migraine had begun to make me nauseous. So before stumbling to my bedroom I made a quick detour to the bathroom, arriving just in time. Pulling myself up from the commode, I used all the energy I had to clean myself up. I've been in that bathroom a thousand times, but for some odd reason, I couldn't find the light switch. Once my fingers located the switch, I heard a noise in the shower. Once again I thought the strange sounds were due to the migraine so I ignored them. As I stared in the mirror to brush my teeth and wash my face before I threw myself in bed, I saw the strangest thing. By now I'd realized what I was seeing and hearing had nothing to do with my migraine.

There was an intruder in my house. Immediately without thinking twice, I pulled the shower curtain back to see where the noise was coming from. What my eyes saw next would forever change my life.

As I stood there looking into the shower, I felt my body go completely numb and then I fell to the floor; almost in a comatose state as I'd observed my own patients do on several occasions.

It was totally weird, I couldn't move or speak; but I was still conscious. By now I couldn't see out of my eye at all. The room seemed to be spinning at 100mph. This feeling was 10times worse than any pain I'd ever had. As I slowly picked myself up from the cold bathroom floor not knowing how long I'd been there I began to replay several scenarios in my mind. Asking myself questions like: Was I dreaming? Where am I? How did I get home? Did I work all morning? Am I that tired? Was this migraine that bad? Is there really a man in my shower? The million dollar question was why are my little girl's underwear in the sink?

Wait a minute. This guy looks a lot like my husband George, but it can't be him. Because he's in our bed watching his favorite show that comes on exactly at 1:30am. I always called George during my 2:00am break, so this just can't be him. Or can it?

Now I get it; someone must have broken in and forced my daughter in the shower. Can someone please wake me because I must be dreaming? No this can't be a dream, because it feels so real. Almost like a living nightmare.

Just as I began to scream I lost all consciousness once again. The next thing that I remembered was being rushed out of the ambulance into the ER.

The truth is, my husband George had been molesting my baby girl for over five years. Almost every night I went to work, he threatened to kill me if my baby girl didn't do what he said. She was his sex slave. I can't believe my eyes were blinded by George's good looks, good sex and his good job. But George was anything but good. Deep down inside, he was a sick monster. Definitely not the man I married.

For the next 48 hours I lay in bed hooked up to an IV, heart, and blood pressure monitors beeping. Or was that noise my heart flat lining from the Sound of TRUTH?

Listen for the warning signs of Abuse:

Physical Signs

- Difficulty walking or sitting
- Bloody, torn, or stained underclothes
- Bleeding, bruises, or swelling in genital area
- Pain, itching, or burning in genital area
- Frequent urinary or yeast infections
- Sexually Transmitted Infections, especially if under 14 years old
- Pregnancy, especially if under 14 years old

Behavioral Signs

- Reports sexual abuse
- Inappropriate sexual knowledge
- Inappropriate sexual behavior
- Nightmares or bed-wetting
- Large weight changes/major changes in appetite

- Suicide attempts or self-harming, especially in adolescents
- Shrinks away or seems threatened by physical contact

SOUNDS OF INNOCENCE

Chapter 5 Sounds of Innocence

Sexual Abuse is an emotional bully.
unknown

Imagine the exciting feeling of recognizing your name for the first time. Counting to ten and memorizing your ABCs. Being able to run and play freely on your own without much help. But before you enter kindergarten, someone comes along and kidnaps your innocence.

Although a sexual abused child isn't physically missing; elements of their young innocent lives are abducted and they will never ever be the same child. Sure they may join the other children in the sandbox, but deep beyond the sand they've buried their soul's secrets. It seems as soon as they let go of mommy's hand and learn how to walk on their own, they stumble into the hands of a predator. A few moments alone with them changes their life forever.

Stop, Drop, and Tell

As an elementary student we often had numerous fire drills. We were told in case of a fire to Stop, Drop, and Roll. I can still visualize that drill in my mind. My classmates and I dropping and rolling on the floor as we followed our teacher's and/or fireman's lead.

As redundant as the drill might seem to a group of giggling third graders, if a fire actually broke out, we knew exactly what to do. After all it was engrained in our tiny little minds with the simple, yet profound life saving tips. If we saw any signs of smoke or fire we immediately knew what to do. Stop, Drop, and yes Roll.

As I reflect back on my childhood days some 30 years ago, I never heard anyone talk about the subject of sex, sexual abuse, incest, molestation, or rape. Or even an in-depth discussion about our fragile innocent bodies. Sex seemed almost like a "don't ask" and surely "don't tell" subject.

Of all the fire drills I participated in, not once do I remember having a fire at school. But as the saying goes, better to be safe than sorry. I was more than prepared how to escape a fire. But what about being trapped in a life constantly filled with heat, fire, and smoke? My life wasn't destroyed by a natural fire, nor did I ever experience third degree burns to my body. However my soul was slowly burned beyond recognition to a pile of useless ashes. Have you ever really looked at a pile of ashes? The color alone is quite depressing and offers no hope.

As a little innocent girl, I felt like I was trapped in a dark burning wooden house, with no windows or doors to escape. The very house which once was used to provide me safety and comfort was the very thing that caused the fire to quickly spread. The absence of windows and doors forced me to suffocate from the smoke fumes which filled every room. I tried to Stop, Drop, and Roll but it was too late.

It was a good practical drill, but it didn't work in reality. Isn't it ironic how people can live right around the corner from the fire station and yet their house can still burn to the ground? Or even worse, their children or pets aren't able to be rescued. Such is the life of any sexual abuse victim. As much as a child maybe under protection and safety from strangers; they somehow still fall prey to evil. Right around their own front doors.

Once I realized what was happening was wrong and that I was being taking advantage of; I immediately spoke out. The smoke signals were evident both inside and outside the house, and the effects of the fire blaze were spreading quickly. Instead of being able to run next door to call 911, I was simply told to put down the phone. Forcing me to keep the fire a family secret.

How do you cover up a fire? the smell, the ashes, and the aftermath? I guess the same way a little 8-year old covers up their internal third degree burns. By forcing yourself to believe that you've never been burned. Sure the hole in the wall is evident but a little paint and dry wall can quickly cover it up. But how does a little innocent child gather up the ashes of their emotions and still live a "Normal" life, both inside and out? Denial doesn't mean that it never happened.

If I could define sexual abuse in a few words, I'd simply say that it's "more than a touch." Rather you've been touched one time or one time too many, its effects have lasting memories and emotional scars that the average person can't begin to fathom. As we teach our kids the fire drills within their schools, let's also teach them to Stop, Drop, and TELL! As parents we teach our kids about many things; strangers, fire safety, gun control, bullying, and drugs. But who is teaching them about the safety zones of their innocent bodies?

What areas are safe to touch? What's the difference between a safe touch and a bad touch? What areas are totally out of reach?

***TELL** until someone listens....*

***TELL** until your story is finally believed.....*

***TELL** until these sick people are sent to prison....*

***TELL** until they're stopped and captured.....*

***TELL** until they're forced to stop hurting and violating*

innocent children....

Stop, Drop, and TELL anyone, everyone,

someone what's going on!

SOUNDS
OF
SUPERMANN

CHAPTER 6 Sounds of SUPERMANN

It is easier to build strong children than to repair Broken Men

Frederick Douglas

1 in 6 men are sexually abused by the age of 18

Truth, Justice, and Freedom

Shortly after the release of my first book, *Inward Scream* I was confronted with a great personal challenge. I began to second guess my decision about releasing the book after a confrontation with one of my close family members. I thought maybe that, I shouldn't have released the book causing my family to endure shame, scrutiny, questions, and judgment. I began to have an incredible war in my mind about what I know I was commissioned to do. Instead of following my heart, I followed what people said and for a moment was gripped by FEAR.

My inner fears went away when one of my male friends shared his personal story with me. Outside of his wife, I was the only other person he'd shared his story of years of sexual abuse with. He picked up a copy of my book his wife had recently purchased. He had no idea what the book was about. After reading it, he was able to share his deepest darkest secrets with his wife of 15years and now openly with me.

It was at this very moment that I knew the release of *Inward Scream* wasn't a mistake. Our meeting in my kitchen was twofold. Drew's confession was as much for him as it was for me. For him it was a safe place to break through years of his silence. And for me, it was a place to break through all the current fears.

In that moment I knew that I must continue sharing my story. In books, emails, newsletters, radio, social media every time I had a chance. I felt that I had written that book just for him. I know for him to share his story with me, was a Bold Step of Faith. You see I wasn't just a stranger who would never see him again; it was a personal friend whom I saw frequently. I knew if I didn't write *Inward Scream* for anyone else, I wrote it for him. By picking up my book, it changed the "Black" S on his chest to a Red one. Taking him from the ashes of his yesterdays to the Red Blood of Jesus that will heal, deliver, redeem, and set him FREE.

As I stared into Drew's eyes, he seem to transform from Clark Kent to Supermann right before for my eyes. His secret was no longer a secret and his Superpowers that day were "Breaking his Silence." To know that my kitchen was used as this Supermann's "phone booth" was riveting.

The day he broke his silence he became SUPER MANN. He shared with me how he was molested for years by his male babysitter. He tried to tell his mother, but she just silenced him even more in her desire to go out partying. He told me how the babysitter started abusing him by sharing marijuana with him, until he slowly adjusted to this dysfunctional lifestyle.

Prior to hearing his story, I didn't personally know any males who struggled with being abused. The pain of sexual abuse isn't limited to a male or female, Pain is still Pain. In fact, 1 in 6 boys are abused by the age of 18. To this day, Drew struggles with many issues including drug abuse. What started out as casual drug use, at hand of his abuser has turned into years of drug abuse and addiction.

The innocence of a young life stolen, masked with being Super cool to smoke marijuana caused a young man to lose his identity. Instead of feeling "SUPER", he feels defeated, shame, lonely, confused—he turns to drugs for comfort to numb his inner pain.

What was silent in the father speaks

in the son and often I found in the son the

unveiled secret of the father.

Friedrich Nietzsche

Facts about Sex Abuse of Males and its Aftermath:

1. Up to one out of six men report having had unwanted direct sexual contact with an older person by the age of 16. If we include non-contact sexual behavior, such as someone exposing him or herself to a child, up to one in four men report boyhood sexual victimization.

2. On average, boys first experience sexual abuse at age 10. The age range at which boys are first abused, however, is from infancy to late adolescence.

3. Boys at greatest risk for sexual abuse are those living with neither or only one parent; those whose parents are separated, divorced, and/or remarried; those whose parents abuse alcohol or are involved in criminal behavior; and those who are disabled.

4. Boys are most commonly abused by males (between 50 and 75%). However, it is difficult to estimate the extent of abuse by females, since abuse by women is often covert. Also, when a woman initiates sex with a boy he is likely to consider it a "sexual initiation" and deny that it was abusive, even though he may suffer significant trauma from the experience.

5. A smaller proportion of sexually abused boys than sexually abused girls report sexual abuse to authorities.

6. Common symptoms for sexually abused men include: guilt, anxiety, depression, interpersonal isolation, shame, low self-esteem, self-destructive behavior, post-traumatic stress reactions, poor body imagery, sleep disturbance, nightmares, anorexia or bulimia, relational and/or sexual dysfunction, and compulsive behavior like alcoholism, drug addiction, gambling, overeating, overspending, and sexual obsession or compulsion.

7. The vast majority (over 80%) of sexually abused boys never become adult perpetrators, while a majority of perpetrators (up to 80%) were themselves abused.

8. There is no compelling evidence that sexual abuse fundamentally changes a boy's sexual orientation, but it may lead to confusion about sexual identity and is likely to affect how he relates in intimate situations.

9. Boys often feel physical sexual arousal during abuse even if they are repulsed by what is happening.

10. Perpetrators tend to be males who consider themselves heterosexual and are most likely to be known but unrelated to the victims.

{This article has been reprinted from MaleSurvivor.org}

SOUNDS

OF

LOVE

Mother May I....

Excuse me Miss, may I have a moment of your time?

Or will it be another one of my senseless crimes?

May I tell you what's really been going on?

Or will you walk again, busy texting and chatting on your phone?

I don't want to lay down another night in fear

Lord please help me not to shed another tear

He always tells me not to utter a mumbling word

But I'm just an eight year old little girl--- still believing in fairy tale world

He touches me in all the wrong places

Causing me to make strange faces

I constantly wet the bed

But no one notices; it's off to work instead

I can't stand his funky smell

But each time he begs me not to tell

It now happens 2-3 times a week
Not knowing what to do I just stay meek

Mother May I....

Tell you to open up your eyes
So you can see his lies

He's very cunning, smooth, and sly
But underneath those pretty brown eyes, he's a vicious spy

I try to give you clues
But I guess his love has blinded you like a fool

I can't stay here anymore with this emotional trauma
I don't know where me and my dolls will live, but not in this drama

Mother May I......
Tell you I'm scared for my life day after day
Can I be a normal little girl who just goes outside and play?

Chapter 7 Sounds of LOVE

There is no fear in love; but perfect Love casts our Fear, because fear involves torment. But he who fears has not been made perfect in love.

1 John 4:18

A Mother's Silence

Parents the greatest gift you can give to your child(ren) is you and your LOVE. Not expensive gifts, clothes, shoes, or even trips to Disney World. Most importantly, they need you and your LOVE. Your child is your most valuable asset. Mothers what price has your children paid for you to hear the "Sounds of Love?"

As little children we've often heard the phrase, "What happens in this house stays in this house." But what if who or what's in the house is bad for you? How does a child survive living in toxic environment?

It's been said that Love is blind, but I'd like to add that Love can also be "Deaf." Love silences its ears to the Truth. The truth when a young innocent child stands before their mother and tells what's been happening to them. Or when the child tries to explain in their very limited vocabulary what their mother's boyfriend or husband has been doing to them. Often behind opened doors. Love becomes deaf to mothers who chose the love of a man over the love and safety of their own child. Or parents so eager to make the next dollar, they don't see the signs of their child's abuse.

Leaving the child feeling hopeless, worthless, and confused about what Love actually is. Unable to differentiate what good love is from bad love, a good touch from a bad touch. When true love is shown they don't know how to receive it. A simple gesture of kindness can make an abused victim question your every motive. Love and trust doesn't come easy to someone whose been abused and often misused all in the name of the Love.

To them your love means their safety and protection, your listening ears and most importantly your open eyes. You must look beyond what you want to see and see the reality of your child's well-being as a #1 priority in your life. Not a man or woman, high paying job, big house, fancy car, or status in the community. Your child is your most valuable asset. Talk with your child openly and honestly about their precious bodies. Teach them about sex, differences between safe and bad touches. Inquire if they've ever been inappropriately touched, and if so; do something about it. No matter who it is, you must confront the silent giant of abuse and speak up and out!

> *When my father and mother forsake me, then the Lord will take care of me. Psalm 27:10*

A Father's Absence

On many Friday nights I spent hours staring out the window, anxiously expecting my daddy's car lights to shine through the window. So I could spend the weekend with him. He would call and say he was on the way. But never showing up or calling. We lived near a busy road so cars were constantly coming and going. Every time I saw or heard a car, I thought it was his.

I would spend most of my early teen years peeking out this window. Waiting on the one man I knew loved me and felt totally safe with. However, he was there but not there. Present but yet absent. Close but yet so far away. I soon adapted to my father's excuses, and eventually his long-term absence.

As a teenage girl, as much as I needed my father's Love it seemed that all I got was his rejection. The more I longed for his attention, the more it seemed he ignored me. In the absence of his attention, I became a very promiscuous young girl. Deep within I knew it was wrong, but I just longed to be loved. Confused Love caused me to look for Love in all the wrong places and faces. By 17, I was pregnant because of the choices I made and as a result of not hearing my father's Sounds of Love for me.

I'm happy to say several years ago my dad and I had a long talk about how his absence affected my life. My dad's absence caused me to blame my abuse on him. It took years for me to realize that I was holding him responsible for other's actions. I forgave him for his absence and how it negativity impacted my life. You must be willing to do the same, Forgive.

I listened for the Sounds of Love in many voices. The absence of my father's voice caused me to scream for attention, validation and affirmation. I listened for Sounds of Love in all the wrong people who told me how much they loved me. But in the end their love hurt me. As a result, Love didn't come easy for me.

My perception of love was so distorted it caused me block out the real "Sounds of Love." Whenever I heard those powerful 4 letters, I questioned the motives behind them. I immediately thought someone wanted something from me. Was it my body, my trust, or my silence?

It wasn't until I heard and felt the unconditional love of Jesus that I knew what real love was. It's meaning, value, and sacrifice. In John 3:16 I learned that God so loved the world that he gave his only begotten son for me. I began to clearly hear the Sounds of Love through the ultimate sacrifice just for my sins. Not only my sins but the sins of my abusers as well.

Love is slow to suspect but quick to trust; slow to condemn but quick to justify; slow to offend but quick to defend; slow to expose but quick to shield; slow to reprimand but quick to empathize; slow to belittle but quick to appreciate; slow to demand but quick to give; slow to provoke but quick to help; slow to resent but quick to forgive.

1 John 4:7

SOUNDS
OF
SEX, LIES, & FAMILY SECRETS

Man is least himself when he talks in his own person.

Give him a mask, and he will tell you the Truth.

Oscar Wilde

Chapter 8 Sounds of Sex, Lies, and Family Secrets

Child abusers thrive in a culture of silence, manipulating, molesting, and controlling children they are sure will never tell

Darwin Hobbs

"Trick or A Treat?"

Many believe that sexual abuse occurs by the hands of total strangers—also known as "Stranger Danger." But in fact 90% of victims know their abusers. Our children are most vulnerable to those they know. Those who sit at our dinner table, sleep in our beds, and have easy access to our innocent children. If people can't be trusted with your personal identification number (PIN), bank account, email passwords, etc., why do we so easily trust them with our children?

My Sounds of sex, lies, and secrets began at age 8 with a simple ride to the store on a hot summer day for ice cream. What started out as a simple ride to the store for a little treat became one of the predator's smoothest tricks. My "Grooming Process" was slowly, methodically, strategically and skillfully planned, one evil step at a time. Most child molesters groom their victims by first gaining their trust. They're chosen carefully; it's a "missing" element that the abusers prey on. They make victims feel special, many who suffer from low self-esteem, are run away children, come from single parent homes, are loners, shy, quiet, etc.

> 90% of victims know their abusers.

They buy the child gifts, make subtle touches, show extra attention and concern, being a mother/father figure to them, allowing the child to get away with things their parents wouldn't approve of. Their small gestures are all intended to feel you out. Find out what you like or don't like, how much you talk or don't. Their plots are like secretly surveying their victims. Giving a child everything they want only to get what they ultimately want from you…trust, secrecy and silence. They strategically create their master plan of manipulation to ultimately control the child.

I remember playing with my older cousins and stopping for a drink at the house of a family friend. Somehow I was accidentally left behind at the house alone with her boyfriend. I probably was there about 30 minutes, but not once did he attempt to touch me. Yet, I was left in the hands of several trusted family members who violated me every chance they got.

Each of my abusers groomed me to gain my trust and keep their dirty little secrets. It started out as extra attention for a young girl who was trying to understand her parent's recent divorce, and seeking a father figure in place of her now absent one.

One of my abusers had long beautiful hair. Every visit to his home ended up with my little cousins and I sitting in his lap. Playing in his beautiful baby doll like hair. What appeared to be innocent child's play was actually a way for him to fulfill his sexual fantasies with little girls. He would give me Mr. Goodbar candy bars all the time, but he was far from "Mr. Good." For my birthday and Christmas I would get extra special gifts from him, most times it was money. For a little girl longing for what other little girls had, the extra dollar here and there was huge. It allowed me to buy the things I saw other little girls' daddy's buying them. I thought I was just extra special to him, one of his favorites. I never knew I'd become a target of his sexual terrorist plot.

I vividly remember the morning his plot all came together, after spending the night at his house with him and his wife. I assume my mom had to do something very important because I rarely spent the night with anyone other than my aunts or dad. But he wouldn't need a night to change my life. One touch, one glimpse, one moment did that for me. As I prepared for what I thought would be a normal school day, I was left me so broken and confused. He showed me, a little 9-year old girl hard core pornography as he forced his tongue in my mouth.

I still struggle with seeing certain images and what appears to be normal love scenes on TV. He implanted a virus in my mental memory bank. And I'm still trying to get rid of those awful memories and images he left on my emotional hard drive. By his awkward touch and the way he made me feel, I knew immediately I needed to tell someone, anyone. And TELL I did. But I was simply told to keep silent about what happened to me, leaving me once again emotionally silent.

My last grooming process started with the gift of two gold rings and lasted for years. He told my mom he found the rings while working outside. Oddly they both fit my fingers perfectly. The rings came long before his first touch. In exchanged I gave him the gift he wanted as well: the gift of my total trust, innocence, and yes my complete Silence.

As I reflect back on that time, those rings symbolized a covenant of secrecy between my abuser and me. The rings symbolized a vow I made to my abuser—to keep his secret "til death do us part, not verbally, but silently. But I decided to divorce all the secrets, shame, and guilt and live totally Free by speaking OUT!

When abusers know you'll keep their secret that's when their true control over you begins. They trick you into believing their behavior is okay. Their attention turns into gifts, their gifts into trust, their trust into touches, pornography, kisses, and their touches into sex. Now you may wonder what a grown man tells a 10-year old girl to lay down with him. The truth of the matter is he doesn't have to tell her anything that he hasn't already told her. He's groomed her into believing that what they're doing is okay. Whenever his behavior is questioned he moves into another level of manipulation and control. Threatening to kill the victim, their siblings or even their parents or grandparents.

Instead of the victim's life being saved, they're tricked into believing that they are saving the lives of others. It's a twisted game of emotional chess as they strategically make their move into the lives of innocent children one sick move at a time.

The Blame Game

Sexual abuse leaves you believing the biggest lie ever told…."It's your fault." Which ultimately leads you on a never ending journey of internal guilt, blame and shame. But how does an 8-year old ask to be physically, mentally, emotionally and psychologically raped?

The blame game says, I caused this to happen to me. I put myself in this situation because I was too friendly, or somewhat flirtatious. I asked for this when I accepted those gifts, money, special favors, or even their extra attention.

Hear me loud and clear. When an adult takes advantage of your childhood innocence, it's not sex; it's sexual abuse. No matter if it feels good to you, causes you to get aroused, erected, or excited; It's Wrong!

Your body was created to feel those things in a natural, healthy and safe way. Not by the hands of a sick sexual predator who has masked their touch as innocent, normal behavior.

When I broke my Silence, I also broke through the secrets of shame, guilt, denial, and condemnation that had followed my life over 25 years. And you, too, can break FREE from these emotional tormentors.

It's not your fault. Forgive yourself and release the blame and shame. Trade your Shame for Courage, Guilt for Freedom, Denial for Truth, and Condemnation for Liberation. My story is now my greatest weapon against the threat of my soul: the silence of Sexual Abuse.

Speaking up and out about what happened to you gives you back your life's control and POWER. As a child, you didn't have control of it being taken away, but you now have total control of your life and freedom.

> *What comforts we should find.*
>
> *If we knew each other's secrets,*
>
> ***John Churton Collins***

SOUNDS
OF
PAIN

Regina L.

The Sounds of PAIN

PAIN it can appear on the brightest of days or peak its head out in the pouring ***RAIN.***

There's something about emotional ***PAIN*** you can't see, hear, or ***EXPLAIN.***

People never know how much it costs you to ***SMILE***

they just expect you to show up and go the extra ***MILE.***

After spending many long nights in ***FEAR,***

you pray maybe your life will change next ***YEAR.***

You try your best to mask your inner ***PAIN,***

but really you're sick and tired of the ***RAIN.***

You pray, cry, vent and even journal but the ink simply ***SMEARS***

from all your ***TEARS.***

You feel your life is not worth ***LIVING,***

and late at night yourself you think of ***KILLING.***

You ask yourself where did I go ***WRONG***?

In this situation I don't even ***BELONG.***

You cry out to everyone, but still no ***RELIEF***;

finally in the hands of God you place all your

BELIEF. He beckons you to come weary, worn, and

ALL; humbly at the feet of Jesus you simply ***FALL.***

Realizing through all your ***WRONG,***

his unconditional love leads right where you ***BELONG.***

The enemy constantly reminds who you were and makes you feel ***ASHAME,***

but in Christ Jesus you are a new creature and **YOU** aren't the ***SAME.***

Don't fret nor ***FEAR,***

God our heavenly father is always ***NEAR.***

He hasn't forgotten about you, don't be tricked by the devil's ***GAME***

God truly loves you and even knows you by ***NAME.***

Chapter 9 Sounds of Pain

Out of suffering have emerged the strongest souls;

the most massive characters are seared with scars.

Kahli

THE

SILENT

SPEAK

"You can accept or reject the way you are treated by other people, but until you heal the wounds of your past, you will continue to bleed.

You can bandage the bleeding with food, with alcohol, with drugs, with work, with cigarettes, with sex, but eventually, it will all ooze through and stain your life.

You must find the strength to open the wounds, stick your hands inside, pull out the core of the pain that is holding you in your past, the memories, and make peace with them"

Iyanla Vanzant

Ann SPEAKS...

I never told anyone about the molestation until now. Between the ages of 7-9 I was touched inappropriately by a male and female cousin on different occasions. Once each time, I don't remember it happening again. At school I was outgoing, overachiever, had to make the dean's list, honor roll every year or I would be devastated. At home I had some attitude problems and difficulty getting along with my sisters. I'm an Extrovert, I believe that blocking out those things at a young age and becoming so involved in school, sports, clubs, and church activities made me busy enough that it was easier to forget what happened. I am comfortable with my personality as an outgoing person now, because I am more confident about myself now.

I've suffered with emotional and self-esteem issues, sexual behaviors (promiscuity) as a young adult, and trust issues have all plagued my life. Memory loss of certain things, it takes certain events to trigger that memory again.

In college I was friendly, outgoing, but not the overachiever, wanted to fit in and do things I couldn't do at home. College became a game, one that I would lose eventually. I began partying and hanging out and meeting all types of men. In college I was raped twice by my male friends. Once after a date and the other incident occurred after attending a study group. My college roommate helped me through the rapes in college.

The rapes occurred by men that I thought liked me, I trusted him enough to go out with him and let him in my home. Dealing with the guilt of if I would have prosecuted, he would have loss his sports scholarship. The last one, I trusted him because he tutored me, he encouraged me as a friend, we studied together, and he betrayed me. I cared for him as a friend and did not prosecute because of the guilt of he would have gone to jail, and may have never graduated from college. These things were shared with my roommate, but never in detail with anyone. So no matter how many men I dated and eventually married, the trust issue continues to be a challenge with men. I have been delivered to a certain level but not to the point I would like to be.

I have been married 2 times. First marriage lasted 2 years and 8 days. It was an abusive relationship, with domestic violence, physical and emotional abuse. The abuse eventually ended my marriage. I did receive counseling for the domestic violence issues. My second marriage is intact but difficult, I'm still trying to overcome trust issues. I've also had to receive counseling due to emotional and trust issues, anxiety and stress in my current marriage.

The issues that stemmed from the molestation plagued me longer than I ever wanted to admit. I never told anyone till now. "Those types of touches that wake up something in a young girl that should not be and then when puberty hits the switch turns back on and never gets turned off."

Jade SPEAKS...

My abuse started at 3 years old at the hands of my brother. The abuse lasted for years and eventually my brother allowed his friends to abuse me as well. I never knew who was going to be in my bed; my brother or one of his friends. I was always quiet and sad as a child but top of my class at school. I ran away at the age of 15 and eventually dropped out of school.

I've been married two times my first husband was a way to get out of the house. He was extremely abusive. I divorced him, and married a much older man, and eventually divorced him too. I have one son, and I did everything possible to raise him exactly opposite of how I wasraised.

When I'm in a business situation, I'm outgoing and friendly. I'm not extroverted at all and don't like being the center of attention. I don't have any close family ties, no long term friends. Nobody knows anything I don't want them to know. Except for the acceptable things in my past, even the people that I talk to in my day to day life know nothing about me.

I still don't trust very many men. I have pretty much stopped dating. I still feel very sad, angered and hurt. It's a daily struggle to bring positive thoughts to the forefront and try to punch the other emotions out.

I've been in counseling at least 4 times maybe 5 over the years. Each time it was good to talk to someone about my feelings and the problems caused by those pent up emotions. But it wasn't until the last counselor that I made some sense of the why of it all. And I think that helped the most with the need to forgive.

L'Dionne SPEAKS…

My step father started sexually abusing me when I was 9 years old. He took me to a motel for the first time at the age of 10. When I asked why he was doing this to me, he said "because I love you." He also told me I was going to be his "little girlfriend" and this was going to be our little secret. As a result of my issues, I had 2 abortions by the time I reached the 11th grade. I'm thankful to say that Jesus has completely healed me from my past and its pain. I once struggled with extreme trust issues, masturbation, pornography, fornication, depression, and suicidal thoughts.

But today I'm FREE! Whenever I see a child with their father I automatically wander if he's abusing them. If I hear a child crying I automatically think someone is hurting them. Images sometimes haunt me of children being abused. My not being able to do anything terrifies and angers me. I am very protective of every child that's around me. I feel it's my responsibility to protect them.

Maria SPEAKS....

I was a little 12 year old girl who quickly learned the only way to get him to stop touching me was to fake my menstrual cycle. While others dread their time of the month, I was Super excited to see mine and somewhat sad to see it end. It was the only time my uncle didn't touch me. So I quickly learned how to fake my time of the month. It became somewhat like an emotional or physical recess for me.

At 13 years old, I thought I was pregnant with my uncle's baby. It was this freighting truth that forced my aunt to break her silence with me. She caught her husband performing oral sex on me in my sleep. Somehow he convinced her that it was a one-time incident and would never ever happen again. Neither one of us moved out of the home, we all were forced to cover up the truth with our silence. We lived in the midst of this new normal life which consisted of many family secrets. We carried them everywhere we went to church, school, family functions and even on vacation. I enjoyed our various road trips because it exposed me to a new environment, perspective, people and I didn't have to guard myself from being touched. Like my menstrual cycle, the vacations offered my body, soul, and spirit a much needed break. But as soon as we returned home, everything would return back to what I call my "dysfunctional normal."

I would still be living in that dysfunction had it not been for the redeeming power of Jesus healing my inner pain. I'd like to tell other victims to deal with their abuse. Or it will eventually deal with you, causing you to slowly commit an emotional suicide.

Mia SPEAKS....

To my knowledge the abuse started when I was 3 or 4 years old. It went on for about a year or so. It happened to me as well as my childhood male friend. The molester was a female. She was actually my mother's good friend's daughter.

I didn't tell anyone until attending a church service where the preacher asked who had been abused or had secrets. I had to be about 13 or 14 yrs of age. I really didn't get counseling, due to my mom being so devastated that she just found out and so did an entire church at the same time. It was a emotional night, I might add.

I haven't been married, I think the incident had a lot to do with it. I've always battled silently, the homosexual spirit, due to being invited in by this woman. I acted out on it once years ago, and was so ashamed afterwards it never happened again. I find myself very protective and alert at all times of EVERYTHING that goes on around me and my children.

My internal problems were battling the homosexual spirit. In order to do so, I took to men x10. Meaning the more men I had in my life, the better I felt about myself. It didn't have to be sexual either. Just knowing they were caught up in me, was enough. I found myself being beat, mentally and physically, and felt I deserved it, because of what had happened to me.

I have always felt like an alien, like I never fit in. I would use my looks to get what I want. I would use my manipulation to work a room and present myself to be someone I totally was not. I was used as a door mat. Then I was taught the game of the world, and hustled it to the fullest.

I found myself rocking in a dark corner at times, even as an adult. I attempted suicide a few times, but I would wake up the next day and became angry. I felt I didn't deserve to be here.

Michelle Speaks…..

A relative sexually abused me when I was about 5 years old. It happened more than once, but because I was a child, I didn't have enough concept of time to say the period the abuse occurred over. He told me if I told anyone that he would kill my siblings.

Since I was a child and by the time I was an adult, I accepted what happened wasn't my fault. As I child, I lied from time to time and stole before I told my adopted mother what happened. I had trust issues also.

The abuse and staying with my biological mother caused my personality to change. I was an extrovert before the abuse and have been an introvert since then. Although I can be extroverted at times.

When I stayed with my biological mother where the abuse occurred I ran away from her house. I was quiet in school, overachiever, on honor roll. When I realized what had happened, I was upset. My biological mother talked to me about it, but the memory haunted me from time to time.

Rita SPEAKS...

I don't remember when abuse actually started. I've been touched, raped and/or molested for as long as I can remember. Once I found out what a virgin was, I knew I wasn't one. To this day the abuse hasn't stopped. I'm currently dealing with spiritual abuse and it feels like I'm being raped all over again.

My Mother always accused me of lying when I attempted to talk about being abused. I knew most of my abusers but was also brutally raped by a total stranger. My abusers were family members, my mother's boyfriends, and even my preacher. I was forced to minimize how abuse made me feel bad. Always made to feel like I was lying. People that knew couldn't say anything about it, but everybody had "Big" finger in front of their lips. Their abuse seem normal to me at the time because I was so accustomed to being touched by someone.

During an recent argument with my Mother, she admitted that she knew what was happening me at the hands of her boyfriends; but needed her bills paid. Through all the pain, I finally had enough courage to forgive my mother earlier this year. It was so freeing!

As a child I was competitive, smart, and an overachiever. Over friendly with boys, was a Thom boy, and slept with most of boys I played with. Got involved into many activities to forget about the abuse. I ran away from home at age 11. I had to have something attached to her name. I had to be Rita, the basketball player or Rita the softball player. My name had to be tied to something else in order for me to be validated. I liked the applause and my name in lights. I often find myself always seeking a mother figure.

As an adult I started having sex for money to pay my bills. I've considered myself as a prostitute but not the type you see on the street. But the type who picks up men at a bar. I seem to attract guys that always force themselves on me.

I was married once for 6-7 months. But sexual abuse aftermaths ruined my marriage because I had intimacy and romance issues. I have no children due to being infected with Stds during my childhood. The STDs made me sterile. I remembers frequently going to Ob-gyn as a young girl, but didn't know why.

As a result of my issues, I'm Bipolar and I've tried to commit suicide twice. I can't handle most situations sober, so I smoke weed and drink alcohol to cope, but their use is situational. Counseling did help me, but I still suffer from outbreaks of depression. I'm currently on medication for severe depression and I have frequent suicidal thoughts.

Samantha Clark SPEAKS…

My uncle started abusing me at the age of 5. I did not even remember my abuse until I was 15 and my older sister brought it to my attention and then all the memories flooded my mind. I am an introvert majority of the time. My personality changed to someone that feels at times that others want to take something from me and might try to hurt me in some way not just sexually.

I was very withdrawn and didn't trust any black males. I was a great student in elementary but when I got to middle and high school I began to not care about grades or my conduct. I did have a group of friends that I only talked to. I did not trust others outside that circle. I ran away from home at 14.

When my ex-husband would touch me in certain areas I would cringe and didn't enjoy intercourse until almost three years into the marriage. I had my first child in my early 20s. I don't let my children stay with family members that are not my sisters or my brothers. No extended family members can keep them even if I trust them.

I have a difficult time since my divorce in trusting another man around my children, someone who is not their biological father.

Shearlie Mae SPEAKS...

I experienced incest at the hands of my uncle at age 5, and it didn't stop until I was 15. I was also sexually abused by one of my aunt's drunken friends—I was 8 at the time. I ran away from home when I was 9 years old. My grandmother permitted a 33-year old seasonal boarder to pay her to have sex with me, I was 13 and a virgin. I slowly and painfully walked to the police department and reported the incident. As I did when my uncle raped me at the age of 15.

At the age of 16, I was placed in a foster home. My foster mother main goal for all 15 of us, was to re-establish our self-esteem. By the time I graduated I knew that I could do accomplish any goal. (In fact I was the first black female allowed to model in Charleston's yearly affair.)

The abuse made me very protective of my children and I made a promise that they would never suffer like I did. I made sure they had the freedom to discuss ANYTHING and EVERYTHING with me.

My past abuse affected my marriages and close relationships. I've been married 6 times, each lasted for 1-10 years. It is my personal opinion that one can use abuse as a weapon to become strong, independent and if it's a generational curse—let it end with you.

Stephanie SPEAKS...

My abuse started at age 5 and it stopped at 13. Yes, incest did occur. Oftentimes, children call it playing house or doctor. I was molested by different people, from family members to friends of the family.

I didn't tell. The day after revealing it to my mother, at 29 years old, I spoke publicly about it in front of hundreds of people.

I was a great student, from elementary school through high school. I had some trouble during my first year of college, more because I was being rebellious and acting out my hurt and pain, but I went on to do very good in college.

I am married and have been for eight years. I have a wonderful husband and marriage. It's special. Everyone says that our marriage encourages them in their relationships. I had intimacy problems early on, as well as fear and trust issues, but that's all in the past.

I don't have any children yet. We plan to have children in the future. I have had abortions as a teen and young adult. Teen pregnancy and abortion is a sure sign of child molestation.

I spent years facing this issue head on, with acceptance, prayer, and forgiveness.

I'm definitely an extrovert. I think the abuse made me crave attention. I've learned to put it into perspective and its proper place. I believe the abuse caused me to have low self-esteem and therefore I was always in competition with other people. I never used to feel good about who I was created to be. I had to reprogram my mind.

There are millions of people suffering from child molestation who don't even realize there's something wrong. The side effects have a way of appearing normal – as if they're just another part of life and things that people go through. I thought my life was fine. I was wrong. I didn't associate my retail/shopping therapy, overspending/ debt, drug and alcohol abuse, criticism and judging of other people, and many other issues, to the abuse. For example, I had to learn that my past problems with men were because of me and how I felt about me not because "all men are dogs" as I'd been falsely told. It was me. It was me. It was me living out the pain of past.

I've been able to sum my healing process up into three words: God. Choices. Change. I put God first. I make better choices. I changed my lifestyle.

SOUNDS
OF
FORGIVENESS

Emotional pain is to the spirit what

physical pain is to the body

Bishop T.D. Jakes

Forgiveness is unlocking the door

to set someone free

and realizing you

were the prisoner.

Max Lucado

CHAPTER 10 Sounds of FORGIVENESS

All bitterness, anger, wrath, insult and slander must be removed from you along with all wickedness. And be kind and compassionate to one another, forgiving one another just as God also forgave you in Christ

Ephesians 4:31-32

Our greatest example of Forgiveness is when Jesus spoke, "Father, forgive them for they know not what they do." Wait…how could this be? Their treatment of him was intentional, purposeful, and downright brutal. They did not accidentally hit him or stepped on his toe. With each strike of his precious body, it was for the intended purpose of causing him Pain, shame, and hurt. It was to "silence" him, his message, his mission, and his purpose. But little did his abusers know, he was sent from eternity into time to fulfill this Mission, which seemed Impossible. I'd be the first to admit, sometimes forgiveness isn't easy. But Jesus made it seem so simple. How did he do it? By forgiving just as God forgave us.

While watching an episode of Hoarders television, I observed a connection between compulsive hoarding and unforgiveness. The man featured on the show became a hoarder after his mother's died. He was so traumatized by his mother's death that he left the calendar from July 1982 hanging up on the wall. It was now twenty years later. Just as the calendar stayed on the same year, so did he. He couldn't move beyond that painful experience. As a result of his grief, he started hoarding. Compulsive hoarding impairs mobility and interferes with basic activities, including cooking, cleaning, hygiene, sanitation, and even sleeping.

The effects of sexual abuse leads one to emotional hoarding. Holding onto years of unnecessary pain, guilt, shame, and unforgiveness only hinders you from living a life of total Freedom. Are you an emotional unforgiveness hoarder? Are you still holding onto past hurts, anger, and pain?

When will you let go of the pain, guilt, shame, condemnation and unforgiveness that no longer serve a purpose in your life? They're just taking up wasted space in your life and cluttering your future.

Releasing the emotional clutter will free up everything that you need. Peace, joy, trust, love, happiness, and Freedom. In order to give ourselves completely away to God and others, we must first be FREE within ourselves….

Part of the show is to help the Hoarder clean up their living areas and get rid of all unnecessary stuff they've accumulated over the years. Today I offer you my help, but the first part of admitting your issue is being real with yourself and confronting your issues.

Ask yourself:

Why do I hold onto the pain?

Why do I choose to hold onto grudges and unforgiveness?

How far will it get me in life?

How will it benefit my future?

As a hoarder, it's hard to see and think clearly when you're surrounded by clutter. Instead of dealing with it, it becomes easier for you to walk around it and ignore its existence. Choosing to wash dirty dishes in a bathroom sink because you no longer have access to a kitchen sink. Pain is the same way; it causes you to ignore the obvious and tell yourself it's not that bad. When confronted with truth about your behavior, you become offensive, often unwilling to change. You fail to realize this causes us to act like that 8-year-old abused child all over again. You feel the need to control your play area because it's "Safe" for you there. But I encourage you to tear down the emotional walls abuse has caused you to live in and freely share yourself with others. Love and be Loved, Forgive and be Forgiven.

Of all the sounds you've heard throughout this book, Sounds of Forgiveness is the most powerful sound you can make. Today, I offer you a chance to release the Sounds of Forgiveness to those who hurt you. Start a journal, reading your bible, reading self-help books like this, joining a support group. These simple things will bring you so much peace, both inwardly and outwardly. As Les Brown so eloquently puts it.....

"Forgiving is not forgetting, it is remembering without Anger."

On January 14, 2007, I stood face to face with one of my abusers. As awkward as it seem, I finally realized I had to let the Sounds of my Forgiveness be heard. As I stood there staring him in the eyes, I felt the Sounds of God's unconditional love working through me. In that moment, I released all the abuse, hurt, pain, shame, guilt and confusion caused by him. The choice to forgive and let go was in my hands. I no longer wanted to be a Sexual Abuse's victim; I wanted to live as a Victor of sexual abuse.

As I released the Sounds of Forgiveness, I also told him that I was never going to be silent about sexual abuse again. As I walked away that January day, I praised God for letting me hear the sweet sounds of his Amazing Grace within the depths of my soul.

Maybe you're reluctant about coming face to face with your abusers, that's totally understandable. However you decide to forgive them is your choice, but forgiveness is a must. You must be willing to give all your hurts over to God and allow him to completely heal you.

The reality is the poison of unquenched anger doesn't infect the perpetrator but only incarcerates the victim. Unforgiveness denies the victim the possibility of parole and leaves them stuck in the prison of what was, incarcerating them in their trauma and relinquishing the chance to escape beyond the pain. {Excerpt from Let It Go-TD Jakes}

Forgiveness FREES you from the painful prison cell others sentenced you to.

Live to Forgive.....Forgive 2 Live

I've personally found so much Freedom in sharing my story with others. Each time I boldly open my mouth to tell others about the Freedom I now walk in I gain another level of confidence. I know without a doubt despite all the pain I've had to endure; this is my Life's PURPOSE.

It's often through painful situations that our greatest strengths are revealed. Don't hoard your pain another day. Don't allow it to clutter your space. FREE your mind, body, soul, and spirit. From this moment forward, choose to be who God created you to be.

Where the spirit of the Lord is there is Freedom

2 Corinthians 3:17

Ten Principles of Forgiveness

Forgiveness begins when you…

1. Accept that life is not fair and that others may play by a different set of rules than you do.

2. Stop blaming others for your circumstances.

3. Understand that you cannot change the person who hurt you; you can only change yourself.

4. Acknowledge the anger and hurt that some unpleasant or even harmful event is causing you.

5. Reframe your story of hurt-your "grievance story'- by placing the hurtful events in a broader context than your current point of view.

6. Recognize that only you can make the choice to forgive.

7. Shift your view of the offender by humbly choosing to empathize with his or her life situation.

8. Intentionally move from discontent toward contentment.

9. Understand that forgiveness will take time and cannot be rushed.

10. Take responsibility for your life and your future....
    {Excerpt from book: *Forgive to Live*}

It's been over 25 years since I first encountered sexual abuse. Sadly over the years a lot hasn't changed when it comes to dealing with sexual abuse. Why are we still discussing this same issue? Why are we still silent about the truth? Our children deserve for us to break our silence, speak the truth and then do something about it.

What do we think our silence will conquer; protect predators or hide our family secrets? Why do we turn our heads while the truth is staring us in our face? While the souls of innocent children are being shattered touch by touch.

You may ask, how do we stop this silent social epidemic? The answer is simple, we stop it by speaking up and out about what we know, see, suspect, and hear.

With courage I have shared my story as well as the story of others. Now go and boldly tell yours.....

Break the Sounds of Silence!

You don't have to forget it to forgive it.

Bishop T.D. Jakes

The scriptures and resources listed below will help you towards your journey of new found Healing, Hope, Joy, and Freedom:

1 John 1:7

2 Corinthians 5:17

James 1:21

John 8:32

Romans 6:4

Matthew 5:44

Philippians 1:6

Philippians 3:13-14

1 John 3:2

John 10:10

Galatians 5:1

Isaiah 61:1-7

Mark 5:34

Jeremiah 17:14

Psalm 15:2

Psalm 147:3

Luke 13:11-13

RESOURCES

Child Help

Website: www.childhelpusa.org

Darkness to Light

Website: www.darkness2light.org

FLORIDA DEPARTMENT OF CHILDREN & FAMILIES

Phone: 1-800-96-ABUSE

Website: www.dcf.state.fl.us/abuse/report/

Florida Council Against Sexual Violence

Website: www.fcasv.org

JUSTICE FOR CHILDREN

1155 Connecticut Ave., N.W. 6th floor

Washington, DC 20036

Phone: 202-462-4688

Website: jfcadvocacy.org

National Children's Advocacy Center

Website: www.nationalcac.org

NATIONAL CHILDREN'S ALLIANCE

516 C St. NE

Washington, DC 20002

Phone: 800-239-9950

Website: nca-online.org

RAPE, ABUSE & INCEST NATIONAL NETWORK

200 L St. NW Ste 406

Washington, DC 20036

Phone: 800-656-HOPE(4673)

Website: rainn.org

THE NATIONAL CRIME VICTIM BAR ASSOCATION

2000 M St. N.W. Ste 480

Washington, DC 20036

Phone: 800-FYI-CALL

Website: ncvc.org

Stop It Now: The Campaign to Prevent Child Sexual Abuse

Website: www.stopitnow.com

SCESA -Sisters of Color Ending Sexual Assault

Website: www.sisterslead.org

Survivors of Incest Anonymous

Website: www.siawso.org

Contact Information:

Regina L. Peeples

Author, Speaker, Sexual Abuse Advocate

I Aministries | PO Box 114 | Fruitland Park, FL 34731

Email: iamminstries@aol.com

Website: www.helpenterprisesinc.com

Therefore I say to you, her sins, which are many, are forgiven, for she loved much. But to whom little is forgiven, the same loves little." Then He said to her, "Your sins are forgiven." Then He said to the woman, "Your faith has saved you. Go in Peace"

Luke 7:47-50

www.ingramcontent.com/pod-product-compliance
Lightning Source LLC
Chambersburg PA
CBHW081217020426
42331CB00012B/3040

* 9 7 8 1 5 9 0 9 4 2 5 1 2 *